BEETLE
SOUP

BEETLE SOUP

AUSTRALIAN STORIES AND POEMS FOR CHILDREN

compiled by
Robin Morrow

illustrated by
Stephen Michael King

SCHOLASTIC
SYDNEY AUCKLAND NEW YORK TORONTO LONDON

Beetle soup: Australia stories and poems for children.

ISBN 1 86388 592 7

1. Children's poetry. Australian. 2. Children's stories. Australian.
I. Morrow, Robin, 1942–.

A820.809282

First published in 1996 by Scholastic Australia Pty Limited
ACN 000 614 577, PO Box 579, Gosford 2250.
Also in Sydney, Brisbane, Melbourne, Adelaide and Perth.

Reprinted in 1997 (twice).

Typeset in 10.7 pt Sabon.

Printed by Tien Wah Press (Pte) Ltd, Singapore.

9 8 7 6 5 4 3   7 8 9 / 9

INGREDIENTS

HOW MANY MILES TO LILYDALE?

Stephen Grey

'How many miles to Lilydale?
    O, wise old walking man:
With your brown, brown face and tired eyes,
    And your stick and billy-can.'

'How many miles to Lilydale?
    'Tis many miles away;
Too many miles for little feet
    To travel in one day.'

'How many miles to Anywhere?
    O, tell me if you can.'
'The road is long and hills are far,'
    Said the wise old walking man.

'Take me away to Anywhere,
    O, wise old walking man.'
But he shook his head as he walked away,
    With his stick and billy-can.

Morning and Evening

Gwendda McKay

I like the two ends of day,
the going out and the coming in of light,
the ending of day and the ending of night.
Each end is a beginning.
Gently the night moves back
and becomes somehow less black,
until
it's cool
and still
and morning.

Night waits all day,
light wants to stay,
but at last birds noisily nest,
the air shivers,
the sky quivers to golden pin points,
until
it's cool
and still
and evening.

THE BATHROOM BUNYIP

Colin Thiele

There's a bunyip in our bathroom,
A creature strange and rare,
We haven't really seen him
But Tom insists he's there.

When the bathroom floor's awash
From our watery aftermath
He says, with cheeky chuckles,
'The bunyip's had a bath.'

When suds pour everywhere
His wit has still more scope:
'Sure, the bunyip's had a bath
And he's used up all the soap.'

When the drainpipe overflows
It's the bunyip's fault again—
'He's fallen down the plughole
And blocked the outlet drain.'

Until at last Mum's patience
Is an overflowing cup:
'The bunyip now,' she thunders,
'Will do the cleaning up.'

THE HIPPOLOTTAMUSS

Nan Hunt

Geoffrey had it all planned.
The box was under his bed, with some twine to tie the lid on. He had poked holes all round the box with scissors.

Thomas-Across-the-Street was happy to go. The big marmalade cat really belonged to Mr and Mrs Mason, but spent most of his time with Geoffrey because there were shrubs in the garden for him to sleep under, and Geoffrey knew just where he liked being tickled and stroked.

Under the weeping elm, in the yard where it was cool and secret, Geoffrey had told Thomas, 'Now Dad's gone, Mum and Jane and me—we have to go away from here to live in the city, you see, and the big van is coming to take all the stuff, but you can come in the car.'

Thomas yawned and purred.

When the van arrived, his mother was too busy to notice what Geoffrey was doing until she called him to get into the car. 'What's in the box?'

'Thomas-Across-the-Street.'

'You can't take him! For one thing he doesn't belong to you, he belongs to the Masons, and for another thing pets are not allowed in the unit. Hurry up and take him back.'

It wasn't the kind of farewell Geoffrey or Thomas would have liked, and Thomas was offended and disappeared quickly when he was let out of the box. In the car, Geoffrey was very quiet. He refused to cry, but the tears ran down inside him and made his stomach ache.

After the first week in the town house when the family was settling down to their new surroundings, Geoffrey brought home the Hippolottamuss. He made a bed for it beside his own and insisted it should be fed.

He was forever saying, 'Look out, you're treading on the Hippolottamuss,' or, 'You can't sit on that chair, that's where the Hippolottamuss is asleep.'

'I can't see it,' said his sister Jane. 'There's nothing there at all.'

'There is so, and he doesn't like being sat on.'

The family put up with it for a week, thinking it would go away, but the Hippolottamuss stayed.

He needed to be taken outside.

He needed the television on to keep him from being bored.

He needed 'his special space', and his own dish of water on the bathroom floor.

'It's all in your mind, Geoffrey,' said Jane. 'It's only an imaginary pet.'

'The Hippolottamuss is not a menagerie pet. He's real and he's mine and he's here.'

After a fortnight the family was desperate. The Hippolottamuss was taking over their lives. 'That beast has to go,' his mother said. 'Please, Geoffrey, take him out and lose him.'

'That would be cruel, and you told me never to be cruel to animals.'

'But he's not a real animal, Geoffrey.'

'Of course he is! He's as real as you and Jane and—and Dad.'

'That's enough, Geoffrey. He can't live here.'

But the Hippolottamuss stayed.

At last Geoffrey's mother rang up Granny, who laughed. 'I'll send Gramp over,' she said.

As soon as he arrived, Gramp went looking for Geoffrey. 'Are you going to introduce me to the Hippolottamuss?'

'Perhaps, Gramp. If he feels like it. You can come with me to where he is, if you like.'

'What's his name, Geoffrey?'

'Tom—no, Billy. Yes, Billy is his name.'

'Can you draw me a picture of him?'

'Yes, yes!' Geoffrey ran to get paper and textas. Gramp sat on the floor and watched while he drew two orange circles, a long curly tail, and some whiskers.

'That's a good colour. I like it. He reminds me of someone I know. Don't tell me, I know! Isn't that Thomas-Across-the-Street?'

Geoffrey nodded, and suddenly he was in his Gramp's lap and crying tears on the outside of his face that helped take away some of the lonely missing-Thomas-very-much ache in his inside.

IT'S WORSE THAN WEEVILS

Norman Lindsay

It's worse than weevils, worse than warts,
It's worse than corns to bear.
It's worse than havin' several quarts
Of treacle in your hair.

It's worse than beetles in the soup,
It's worse than crows to eat.
It's worse than wearin' small-sized boots
Upon your large-sized feet.

It's worse than kerosene to booze,
It's worse than ginger hair.
It's worse than anythin' to lose
A Puddin' rich and rare.

PLEASE WASH ME UP

Peter Combe

'Please wash me up,' said the knife,
'I'm sticky all over with honey.'

'Please wash me up,' said the plate,
'I'm yucky all over with Weetbix.'

'Please wash me up,' said the glass,
'I'm sticky all over from orange juice.'

'Please wash me up,' said the fork,
'There's egg stuck in my prong.'

'Please wash me up,' said the frying pan,
'I've got fried potatoes stuck on my bottom.'

'Please wash me up,' said the fingers,
'We've got icecream all over us
And we hate being licked!'

THE KING WHO WANTED TO REACH THE MOON

Lilith Norman

There was once a King who had everything he could possibly want. Still he was not satisfied. If only he could prove that he was more important than all the other kings in the world. He thought and he thought, and at last he decided upon a plan. He would climb up and touch the moon. That would prove that he was the greatest king in all the world.

So he sent for the Royal Carpenter. 'You must build me a tower that will reach to the moon.'

'Anything Your Majesty desires,' said the Royal Carpenter, bowing low. He backed out of the King's room, and scurried to his workshop.

'Quick! You must build a tower to reach the sky!' he said to his underlings. 'The King demands it.'

'What shall we build it with?' asked the Second Carpenter.

'Wood, nitwit!' yelled the Royal Carpenter. 'If the King had wanted it of stone, he would have called for the Royal Mason. Quick! Quick!'

The carpenters ran hither and thither, collecting all the logs and planks and timber they could find, while the Royal Carpenter sat up night after night designing the tower. But no matter how much he drew, and planned, and calculated, he couldn't make a tower that would reach the sky.

As the days passed and no tower appeared on the palace lawn, the King became angrier and angrier. At last he sent for the Royal Carpenter. 'Where is my tower?' he screamed. 'If it is not built by tomorrow morning I shall chop off your head.'

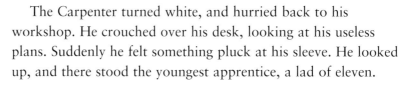

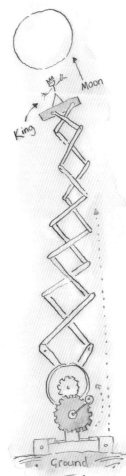

The Carpenter turned white, and hurried back to his workshop. He crouched over his desk, looking at his useless plans. Suddenly he felt something pluck at his sleeve. He looked up, and there stood the youngest apprentice, a lad of eleven.

'Please, your honour, how about piling up boxes? My baby brother builds towers with his blocks like that,' said the apprentice.

'Brilliant!' cried the Carpenter, and he sent out an order for everyone in the land to bring in all the boxes they had. Soon the palace yard was piled with boxes—apple crates, shoe boxes, egg cartons, medicine boxes.

All through the night the Royal Carpenter and his men worked, stacking the boxes one on top of the other, and in the morning, when the King stuck his head out his window, the first thing he saw was a great tower rearing up into the sky.

Still in his dressing-gown the King rushed downstairs, his slippers flip-flapping. He shaded his eyes and gazed up to where the tip of the tower disappeared behind some clouds.

'Excellent, excellent,' he exclaimed. 'I shall go up at once.'

'But sire, don't you think it looks a little shaky,' said the Royal Carpenter. 'Perhaps I should go up first, to see if it is safe.'

'You forget yourself, Carpenter,' said the King. 'No one shall touch the moon but me. Out of my way.' He shoved the Carpenter aside and began to climb. Up and up he went, till at last he stood, swaying, on the very topmost box. He reached out his fingers, but the moon was just centimetres away. 'I need one more box!' he called down.

The Royal Carpenter stared in dismay. There was not a single box left anywhere in the kingdom. 'There are no more boxes, Your Majesty,' he called up.

'Nonsense!' yelled the King. 'Take the bottom box and send that young apprentice up here with it!'

'The—the—bottom box, Your Majesty?' stammered the Carpenter.

'You heard me!' bellowed the King.

So the Carpenter pulled out the bottom box. Down came the tower. Down came the King. Somewhere, amongst all those millions of boxes, is the King— but nobody has found him yet.

THE ANT EXPLORER

C J Dennis

Once a little sugar ant made up his mind to roam—
To fare away far away, far away from home.
He had eaten all his breakfast, and he had his Ma's consent
To see what he should chance to see and here's the way he went—
Up and down a fern frond, round and round a stone,
Down a gloomy gully where he loathed to be alone,
Up a mighty mountain range, seven inches high,
Through the fearful forest grass that nearly hid the sky,
Out along a bracken bridge, bending in the moss,
Till he reached a dreadful desert that was feet and feet across.
'Twas a dry, deserted desert, and a trackless land to tread;
He wished that he was home again and tucked-up tight in bed.
His little legs were wobbly, his strength was nearly spent
And so he turned around again and here's the way he went—
Back away from desert lands feet and feet across,
Back along the bracken bridge bending in the moss,
Through the fearful forest grass, shutting out the sky,
Up a mighty mountain range seven inches high,
Down a gloomy gully, where he loathed to be alone,
Up and down a fern frond and round and round a stone,
A dreary ant, a weary ant, resolved no more to roam,
He staggered up the garden path and popped back home.

FLIES

Irene Gough

Flies! Flies!
They take you by surprise,
They get in your mouth
And they get in your eyes.

Flies! Flies!
Half a hundred tries
To swim in the soup
And dance on the pies.

I spray them and shout at them
You'd think that they would know
They haven't any welcome,
And I wish they'd go!

THE SOCK FUNERAL

Gwendda McKay

Where do they go, those missing socks
Whose widows wait in an odd-sock box?
How did they miss the drip dry spin?
Did we toss them out? Did we leave them in?
Are they stuck in a maze of hoses,
Never again to warm our toeses?
'Lost in the wash,' it's gen'rally said.
Perhaps it actually means they're dead!
Alas and alack, they never come back,
They never come back,
They never come back.

Cheerful Version

Where do they go, those missing socks
Whose partners wait in an odd-sock box?
Tired of warming people's toes
They're off to a land that no one knows.
Reds and blues and stripes and spots,
Greens and yellows and polka dots,
Dancing away to have some fun
Leaving our feet with only one.
Alas and alack, they'll never come back,
They'll never come back,
They'll never come back.

ON RAINY NIGHTS

Anne Bell

Sleep warm,
Though the envious wind fingers the eaves
And the windows are curtained with rain,
The roof stays strong and the wall stands firm,
Sleep warm.

Sleep well,
There's bread in the crock and milk in the jug,
There's fire on the hearth, and the dog and the cat
Are curled like commas there,
Sleep warm, sleep well.

THERE AND BACK

Libby Hathorn

Train leaps forward
silver track
bullet fast
there and back.

I
love the sound
murmur to scream
gnawing and gnashing
on rails that gleam.

When
stations loom
shudder and shake,
slithers to stop
great long snake.

Then
train leaps forward
silver track
bullet fast
there-and-back
thereandback
thereandback
there-and-back.

DAN McDOUGALL AND THE BULLDOZER

Lydia Pender

Dan McDougall lived in the bush, among the ironbarks and the stringybarks and the box-trees, the red gums and the blue gums and the scribbly gums, and all the other eucalypts.

Dan McDougall was only a little man, oh, quite a little man, but he had an enormous friend, and his friend was—a bulldozer.

The bulldozer was very strong, and very heavy, and very, very noisy. He was painted a fine strong yellow, as bright as a pumpkin flower, and he had his name in big, black letters along one side: BULLDOZER MANUFACTURING COMPANY LIMITED. But nobody ever called him that; it was much too long. Dan McDougall always called him Dozer.

Dan lived in a snug little hut he had built for himself under the ironbarks. It had a door at the front and a window at one end. And at the other end it had a small black stove with a tall black chimney, to cook his meals and keep him warm in the wintertime.

Dozer's hut was right alongside Dan's. It had a great, wide door and a window at each end, but no stove at all. 'Dozer never really feels the cold,' Dan used to say.

Dan McDougall liked good tucker, and he liked variety. But Dozer liked a simple diet. 'All he wants,' said Dan, 'is diesel oil. He's very easy to please.'

All the farmers around knew Dan McDougall. Whenever a new dam needed to be dug, or a paddock needed to be cleared, someone would be sure to say:

'Send for Dan McDougall. Dan and his big friend Dozer will have the job done for you as quick as a wink.'

And so they did. As soon as Dan let out the clutch, Dozer would be off, rumbling and roaring with joy and importance:

'Gr-r-rang . . . gr-r-rang . . . gr-r-rang . . .' pushing and shoving a track through a patch of prickly pear;

'Gr-r-rang . . . gr-r-rang . . . gr-r-rang . . .' rattling over clumps of bracken, and crushing them into the mud.

Sometimes there were trees to fell. Dan sat up in the driving seat, pulling his levers and shouting his orders:

'At 'im, Dozer! Get 'im, Dozer!'

'Gr-r-rang . . . gr-r-rang . . . gr-r-rang . . .' and the tree would drop with swishing twigs and crashing branches and great, thudding trunk, leaving its torn and broken roots waving up at the sky.

Dozer was as happy as a magpie. But Dan McDougall dreamed his dreams—of the city that stood by the sea; of its crowded streets, and its towering roofs, and the busy ships on its smooth, blue bay.

One day Dan walked into Ted Donaghue's store and asked a question: 'What would it cost me to get to the city that stands by the sea?'

'It all depends,' said Ted. 'If you thumb a lift with the mailman, when he comes around,' said Ted, 'he'll take you to the railway siding, and the train stops there on Thursdays. Would you be coming back?' asked Ted.

'Oh, I couldn't stay,' said Dan. 'Dozer would be lonely if I left him for long. No, I'll be back,' said Dan.

Old Ted Donaghue thumbed through the timetable, and moved his thick finger slowly down the page. 'One hundred dollars there and back,' said Ted.

Back in his snug little hut, Dan McDougall counted his cash. 'Not enough here,' said Dan. 'It's a pity I can't take Dozer.' And then Dan McDougall had a terrific idea. 'Why shouldn't *Dozer take me*?' he said.

So the very next morning, off they went.

'R-rumble . . . r-rumble . . . r-rumble . . . ' over the soft dirt roads of the blacksoil plains, sleeping at night-time under the sparkling stars;

'Gr-r-rang . . . gr-r-rang . . . gr-r-rang . . . ' over the steep and stony road that wound up the mountain range;

'Gr-angle-angle-angle-angle . . . ' over the zig-zag track down to the coastal plain; and

'R-rumble . . . rumble . . . rumble . . . ' over the smooth, straight road to the city that stood by the sea.

But now the traffic was thickening. Fast cars shot past, tooting them rudely out of the way; buses came hustle-and-bustling by, ringing their jingling bells. And all around them noise hammered and clattered and roared.

Dan was growing confused, and muddling over his levers. Dozer was snorting and stopping and starting, and Dan simply couldn't control him. Then suddenly there they were in the city's central square!

People were everywhere! Shopping mothers, solemn doctors, little whistling boys. Along one side stood the flower stalls, packed with scented blossoms; over the way, the fruit barrows, piled high with rosy apples; and across the square the traffic lights winked and blinked and beckoned, amber to red, and red to green.

Dozer's engine was purring and throbbing. Poor tired Dan let in the clutch, and off rattled the bulldozer, rumbling and roaring with joy and importance:

'Gr-r-rang . . . gr-r-rang . . . gr-r-rang . . . ' Dan McDougall had muddled his levers, and Dozer was clearing a paddock! Scooping up the flower stalls and flinging them on to the footpath! Pushing the fruit barrows into the gutter, like dust in front of a broom!

'Gr-r-rang . . . gr-r-rang . . . gr-r-rang . . . ' People were scampering hither and thither, and squealing like startled rabbits—

'Call out the police! Call out the fire engines! Call out the army!'

'Gr-r-rang . . . gr-r-rang . . . gr-r-rang . . .'

Rosy apples were bouncing and rolling, and flowers strewed the roadway like a royal wedding! Round they roared again, and down toppled a lamppost, with twisted tip and broken globes, and all its silly, snapped-off wires waving up at the sky! And then—

'Gr-romp . . . Gr-romp . . . Gr-r.' With a stutter and a shudder and a shake, Dozer had stopped at last. No more diesel oil!

So Dozer went home in disgrace (and so did Dan). They loaded Dozer on to a trailer, and off they set for the bush. Dan sat in the cabin beside the driver and back they went over the coastal plain; back over the mountain track; back over the blacksoil plains, to the ironbarks and the stringybarks and the box-trees, to the red gums and the blue gums and the scribbly gums, and all the other eucalypts; back home to the bush.

'This is the place for you,' said Dan McDougall, 'and this is the place for me.'

NOW WOULDN'T IT BE FUNNY

Pixie O'Harris

Now, wouldn't it be funny
If the creatures in the Zoo,
Were all let out to walk about
And look at me and you?

And wouldn't it be funny
If they put us in the cages,
And Kangaroos and Cockatoos
Came guessing at our ages.

And wouldn't it be funny
If the Hip-O-Pot-amus
Said, 'Don't go near, I really fear
They're very dangerous.'

The Happy, Sad, Happy Car

Lyn Donald

Once there was a shiny white car with red seats and seat-belts, a radio, a big silver aerial on the bonnet, a shiny exhaust pipe showing at the back and a big, strong engine.

The engine was so strong that it started every morning, even in frosty, cold weather, or the pouring rain. *B-r-r-rum!*

Everyone who looked at it said, 'My word, what a nice car!'

Joe, the man who owned it, was very proud of his car.

Then, one night, the beautiful, shiny white car came out in big, round, black spots. Nobody knew why—whether it was a bad case of car measles, or whether an elephant with a huge trunkful of black paint had sneezed all over the car without putting his hand over his mouth. The spots were there and they would not come off. Joe rubbed and scrubbed, rubbed and scrubbed, but the spots stayed, big and bright as ever.

Now, when Joe drove along the street in his white and black spotty car, people laughed and pointed. He felt very silly. There were lots of fine cars with a stripe on them and even some with writing on them but nobody else had a car with big, black spots on it.

Joe became so cross with the laughing people that he drove 'Spotty' to a car salesyard and traded it in for a beautiful yellow car.

In the salesyard, people looked at Spotty and said, 'Yuk!' They bought red cars, green cars, purple cars, white cars, black cars, orange cars and even gold cars. No one wanted a spotted car.

Then one day, a tall man came in with a dog, the kind of dog called a Dalmatian, a white dog with big, black spots. This one wagged his tail all the time and was as friendly as could be.

The man and his dog looked at red cars, green cars, purple cars, white cars, black cars, orange cars and even gold cars—and said 'Yuk!' to them all. Then they saw the spotted car at the back of the yard. It was covered with dust, but the man rushed over with his spotty dog and nearly jumped for joy.

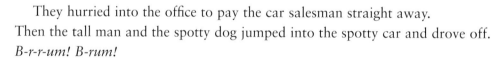

He had found a car he really loved!
The dog wagged his tail as if he loved it too.

They hurried into the office to pay the car salesman straight away. Then the tall man and the spotty dog jumped into the spotty car and drove off. *B-r-r-um! B-rum!*

The spotty car was taken home, washed and polished and put in a big garage. The spotty dog slept in the garage in a big basket alongside the spotty car.

The tall man thought he had the finest car and the finest dog in the whole world.

CITY SONG

Dorothy Rickards

Balancing birds on telegraph wires
Look like the music of my city song—
    City noises, honking, hooting,
    Scraping feet and taxis tooting,
    Ringing bells and voices speaking,
    Rattling tins and tram wheels shrieking—
All make music for my city song.

THE GOBBLERS

Madeline Rose

Mr Trimble was trying to cut the grass, but the lawnmower would not work. He stamped and raged and shouted. His children, Tom and Tess, didn't know what to do.

Just then, a little van, painted all over with flowers, pulled up outside their gate. A small man climbed out. Tess and Tom were surprised to see that his fingers were green.

Greenfingers listened to the shouting, then said to Mr Trimble, 'What you need is gobblegrass. I think I have a pot with me.'

Greenfingers opened the back of the van and pulled out a flowerpot. The plants in it looked like a green carpet.

'Gobblegrass is the thing for you,' he said. 'It never needs feeding or watering or mowing. Just plant it in your lawn. It will spread very quickly.' Then he climbed into his van and drove away.

Mr Trimble dug a hole in the middle of the lawn, and Tess and Tom helped him plant the gobblegrass in a tiny, green circle.

But in the night the gobblegrass grew and grew, smothering the grass around it. In the morning the patch was as big as the lid of a garbage bin. By the next day it had grown as wide as the kitchen table. It spread and spread until it covered the lawn. If Tom and Tess took their shoes off, it felt rough and tickly.

Mr Trimble was delighted to have no more mowing. Mrs Trimble did not like it when it started to cover the flowerbeds, but Mr Trimble said, 'Flowers are too much trouble. We need a no-work garden. Let's just have one big lawn, of gobblegrass.'

The gobblegrass covered the marigolds and the forget-me-nots. It flattened the daisies and the geraniums. Then the gobblegrass crept up the drive and crawled up the trunk of the apple tree. It started to climb fences.

Mrs Jiggs, next door, was worried. 'You must stop that weed,' she cried, 'before it spoils my roses.'

Mr Como, on the other side, was even more alarmed. He shouted, 'Keep that gobblegrass away from my peas and carrots.'

Mrs Trimble and Tess and Tom tried to pull the gobblegrass off the fence, but it stuck faster than glue. Mr Trimble tried to dig it up, but its roots went too deep.

The children went looking for Greenfingers. They found his little van, parked under a tree.

'To get rid of gobblegrass,' he said, 'you need gobbleflies. Luckily I have some with me.'

He gave them a jam jar, which had holes punched in the lid. It was full of fiercely buzzing flies. 'These gobbleflies will fix the gobblegrass,' said Greenfingers. 'They are tiny, but very hungry.'

When the jar was opened, the flies flew out, and began to eat the gobblegrass. They were very hungry indeed. All day long they ate and ate and ate. At night, lying in bed, Tess could hear the noise of gobbleflies, munching gobblegrass.

After seven days only bare earth was left, all over the garden.

But the gobbleflies were still hungry. They began to munch the leaves on the apple tree. They flew into Mrs Jiggs' garden, and started on her roses. They buzzed over the fence to chew Mr Como's lettuces. The neighbours became very angry.

Tom and Tess found Greenfingers' van at the end of the road.

'You do have bad luck with your garden,' he said. 'To get rid of gobbleflies, you need a gobblebird.' And he pulled out a cage which contained a bird with blue feathers and red, scaly legs. It looked at the children with shiny, black eyes and clicked its big yellow beak.

Mrs Trimble did not like the gobblebird at all. Tess opened the door of the cage and out the bird hopped. First it ate the flies on the apple tree. Then it flew over the fence and flapped above Mr Como's vegetables, snapping its beak and hunting gobbleflies. And it whirled over Mrs Jiggs' garden, gobbling the flies upon her rosebushes. All day long it snapped and gulped and swallowed. And at night it roosted in the apple tree.

Two days later, Tom and Tess could not find a single gobblefly.

But the gobblebird was still hungry. It hunted bees and butterflies. It gobbled ladybirds. 'Those ladybirds kept my roses free of greenfly,' cried Mrs Jiggs.

Mr Como shook his fist at the bird. 'If it eats all my bees, we shall have no honey.'

Tess and Tom shouted and flapped their arms, to try to scare the gobblebird away, but it took no notice.

In the middle of the night, as the gobblebird slept in the apple tree, Mr Trimble fetched his ladder. Very quietly he began to climb.

But when he reached out to grab the gobblebird, it woke and squawked and pecked him on the nose. And he fell off the ladder.

Next morning the neighbours came round to complain. 'It's all your fault!' they said to Mr Trimble. 'First that grass, and then those flies, and now this horrible bird. You must do something about it!'

Suddenly there was a knock at the door, and who should it be but Greenfingers, carrying a large basket!

'I like to make sure my friends are happy,' he said. 'Did the gobblebird eat your gobbleflies?'

'Yes, it did,' wailed Mrs Trimble, 'but it won't stop eating. We shall soon have no bees or butterflies. Will you please take it away?'

'I am so very sorry! I was only trying to help,' said the little man.

'Can you catch that bird for us?' asked Tom. 'No, no,' said Greenfingers. 'Nobody can catch a gobblebird. They are far too quick and clever.'

'Then what are we going to do?' cried Mr Trimble.

'The only thing that can catch a gobblebird,' said Greenfingers, 'is a gobblecat. By the greatest good fortune, I have one in my basket.'

He opened the lid of the basket and the gobblecat leapt out. It was five times as big as an ordinary cat. It had black fur, striped with yellow, and long tufts on its ears. It smiled at Tess and Tom, showing big, sharp teeth.

'Now wait a minute,' gasped Mrs Trimble. 'That animal looks dangerous.'

'No, no,' laughed Greenfingers, 'They make wonderful pets. And it will fix your gobblebird very quickly.'

The gobblecat prowled about the garden, stalking the gobblebird. Some time during the night, the gobblebird vanished. Did the gobblecat scare it away? Or did it gobble it up?

The gobblecat did not make a good pet. Tom and Tess did not dare to stroke it. It was so big. It had such sharp teeth and claws. It had a very peculiar smile.

And it was always hungry. No matter how much food they gave it, it always asked for more.

And now that the gobblebird had gone, the gobblecat hunted other birds. It could leap high into the air. It moved silently and gobbled sparrows, parrots, wrens and finches. Crunch, munch and they were gone, and the gobblecat licked its lips.

The gobblecat sat watching Mr Como's chickens, and smiled its greedy smile. Mrs Jiggs did not like the way the gobblecat looked at her baby.

'Everyone is angry with us,' said Mrs Trimble. 'That gobblecat has to go.'

But they could not catch the gobblecat. It hid in trees and under bushes, and caught more birds than ever.

'It's all the fault of that Greenfingers,' complained Mr Trimble.

Tess and Tom went out again to search for him. At last they found him, near a round-about, and he was eating his lunch.

Greenfingers listened to their story, laughed and said, 'What you need is a gobbledog. And luckily I can let you have one.'

'No!' said Tom.

'No!' said Tess. 'We don't want a gobbledog.'

'You never meant to help,' said Tom. 'You were only playing tricks. We don't want any more of your gobblers! Because of you, our garden is all spoilt. There are no bees or birds. And all our neighbours are angry.'

'Ah well,' said Greenfingers, 'I'll try to put things right.'

When they got home the gobblecat seemed pleased to see Greenfingers. It did not struggle at all when he popped it into his basket.

In the back yard, Greenfingers looked around him. There was no lawn at all. The gobblegrass had killed the grass, and the gobbleflies had eaten the gobblegrass. There were no flowers or leaves.

'Dear me!' said Greenfingers. 'I shall have to do something about it.'

Just then it started to rain, splashing on the bare ground. 'Now we shall have nothing but mud,' said Tess.

'This is just the right weather,' he said, 'for sowing my magic seeds. We will fix this garden. It will be a big surprise for your parents.'

He pulled some little bags out of his pockets, red and yellow, pink and blue. He capered around in the rain, tossing seeds all over the garden, and Tom and Tess joined in the fun. Then he ran back to his van and drove away.

The seeds sank into the soft mud. Then it grew dark outside and the children could see nothing.

Next morning they had a garden again. They had a fine, green lawn, and hundreds of flowers. Mr and Mrs Trimble cried, 'However did it happen?'

After a while new birds and insects found the new garden. Bees buzzed, and honey-eaters sipped nectar from the blossoms.

Tess and Tom smiled. And they never saw Greenfingers again.

TOO EARLY

Gordon Winch

Early to bed
and early to rise
makes a man healthy,
wealthy and wise.

Birds prosper too,
if they're quick out of bed;
It's the earliest bird
who is the best fed.

But think of the worms
on which birds dine and sup.
They'd be much better off
if they didn't get up.

GARDENING DAY

Joan M Shilton

Digging, digging, digging
Underneath the hedge,
Pulling all the weeds out,
Tidying the edge.

Breaking, breaking, breaking
Great thick clods of dirt.
Mustn't hit a finger—
That can really hurt!

Wriggling, wriggling, wriggling,
See the long thin worms
Sweetening the garden
With their twists and turns.

Planting, planting, planting
Seeds so small and round,
Into cosy darkness,
Hidden in the ground.

Turning, turning, turning
The tap to fill the hose.
Now we have our shoes wet—
How fast the water flows!

Swishing, swishing, swishing,
Just a gentle spray,
Spurting too much water
Will wash the seeds away.

Waiting, waiting, waiting
For shoots and buds to grow,
Soon a blaze of colour
Flowering row by row.

CORN
FLOWER

WATCHING EYE

Colin Thiele

In the corner of the garden
I noticed something lie
like a little chip of glass
so I gently stooped to pry.

A tiny spider watched me
with a spider's tiny eye.

WHO'LL BUY?

Dorothy Simmons

Puppies for sale! Puppies for sale!
Midnight yappers, sandshoe nappers,
Tennis-ball trouncers, wind-leaf pouncers,
Pocket rippers, big toe nippers,
Wrigglers squigglers, snugglers cuddlers . . .
Puppies for sale! Puppies for sale!

Song of the Months for South Australia

C E C

January brings us peaches and plums;
And in February great heat comes.

In March, the vintage claims our cares,
And apples fall, and dainty pears.

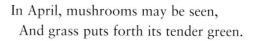

In April, mushrooms may be seen,
And grass puts forth its tender green.

In May, the leaves turn red and brown,
And winds of winter blow them down.

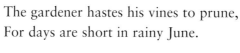

The gardener hastes his vines to prune,
For days are short in rainy June.

The mornings are frosty in cold July,
And oranges ripen and creeks run high.

In August the almonds their blooms display,
Which fall like snow on a stormy day.

The wattle's rich scent on the breeze is borne,
And in September the sheep are shorn.

In lovely October the loquats are sweet,
And lilacs and roses and daffodils meet.

In November the hot wind scorches the plain,
And fields are waving with golden grain.

The days are long, and the heat may weary,
But Christmas makes December cheery.

RAINBOW DUCKLING

Robin Klein

Once there was a little yellow duckling, and his feathers were as clean and as shining bright as a dandelion flower. His mother said proudly, 'You are the finest duckling who ever paddled in this farm's pond!'

One day, the little yellow duckling paddled across the pond and climbed up the far bank. He waddled away to look at new and different things.

Next to the tractor he found a very small pond, the size of a saucepan lid, and he sat down in it. He didn't know it was a patch of oil. When he got up, his tail-feathers weren't yellow any more.

'My tail looks different,' he thought.

Then he found a purple pond in a tin, a purple pond of purple paint. There was room only for his beak in this pond.

'My beak looks different,' he thought, staring at it with his eyes crossed.

The farmer's wife had been using dye to change a dull old tablecloth into a bright blue one. She had pegged it up on the clothes-line. There was a tiny blue lake under the clothes-line. Blue raindrops were falling into it. The duckling dipped his yellow wings into the lake, and they changed from the yellow colour of a dandelion flower to the green-blue colour of the sea.

'My wings look lovely!' he declared.

The farmer's son had been polishing a horse's hooves with some black stuff in a dish. A little black puddle in its own special dish! The duckling dipped first one, then the other webbed foot into the black puddle. He looked down at his feet and thought they looked very smart. It looked as if he had black rubber boots on like the farmer, only very much smaller, of course.

He marched along with his oily tail-feathers, and his purple beak, and his green-blue wings, and his little black boots. He felt very new and different.

The farmer's daughter had picked a bucket of blackberries. The duckling hopped on to the rim of the bucket and jumped in. *Plosh!* What a strange pond it was, with lumpy water that didn't feel like water at all! He climbed squishily out of the bucket and gazed at his tummy. It was covered with squashed blackberries. They looked like buttons.

He went back to the farm's big pond and his mother quacked crossly, 'Who turned my lovely little dandelion-yellow duckling into a patchwork rug?'

She shoo-ed him into the pond and splashed water over him. Soon his tail-feathers were yellow again. His feet lost their little black boots. His wings changed from the colour of the sea to the colour of a dandelion flower. The blackberry buttons floated away in the water.

'There!' said his mother proudly, as she cleaned the last streak of purple paint from his beak. 'You're the finest duckling who ever paddled in this farm's pond!' she quacked.

But the little yellow duckling quite enjoyed being a rainbow, and thought that tomorrow he might go out and look for those lovely patchwork puddles again.

THE CARETAKERS

Anne Bell

I went to the house, looking for a man to build a fence,
Knowing nothing of him, except that people said
He built good fences.
His garden warmed July's cold hills,
But there was nobody there,
Save a peacock, a scarecrow and a fine grey mare.

I found nobody to build my fence,
But I think I'd like a man
Who left his home to the care
Of a peacock, a scarecrow and a fine grey mare.

THE LITTLE THINGS

Anne Bell

On nights when storms run wild,
And thunder tramples the stars,
When lightning startles the wakeful eye
Pity the little things;
The soft-breasted pigeon, rocked
On a brittle nest of too-few sticks;
Wren and thornbill and finch;
All creatures crouched in bending crops;
Hare and mouse and freckled quail;
All things that have no roof save storm—
On nights like these,
Pray for the little things.

COMING HOME

Joan M Shilton

Driving home in the car
Cosy and warm
Through the storm.

Wipers pierce the beads
Of curtained rain
Again and again.

Fierce black traffic beasts
Beam to the skies
Their blinding eyes.

Bright traffic lights drip
Red and green streaks
Into road creeks.

Tyres splurt and splash
Zig-zag and swerve
Round the curve.

Huge shadowy limbs
Of trees in the park
Grasp at the dark.

Warm milk by the fire
Safe from the blast
Home at last.

THUNDERSTORM

Robert Wilson

The lightning went flash. The thunder went BOOM.
The wind went WOOOOH and shook the whole room.
Little Lisa and her pet dog Boofy woke up with a fright.
'I'm scared of thunderstorms,' thought Lisa. She quickly got out of her bed and climbed into bed with her big brother, Adam.
The lightning went flash. The thunder went BOOM.
The wind went WOOOOH and shook the whole room.
Adam woke up with a fright. 'I'm scared of thunder-storms,' thought Adam. He quickly took Lisa by the hand and they all, including Boofy the dog, climbed into bed with their big sister, Sarah.

The lightning went flash. The thunder went BOOM.
The wind went WOOOOH and shook the whole room.
Sarah woke up with a fright.
'I'm scared of thunderstorms,' thought Sarah. She quickly took Lisa and Adam by the hand and they all, including Boofy the dog, climbed into Mum and Dad's bed.
'There's not enough room in the bed for all of us,' said Mum. 'Sorry Dad, but you'll have to hop out.' Tired and bleary eyed, Dad staggered to Sarah's bed and plonked down to sleep.
Finally the lightning stopped flashing. The thunder stopped BOOMING, and the wind stopped WOOOOHING. The thunderstorm was over and the house was still.

Sarah was fast asleep until Boofy started scratching.
He scratched so madly that the bed started shaking.
Sarah woke up and said
'Boofy you bad dog!
Boofy you pest!
I'm leaving this bed
to get some rest!'

She climbed out of her Mum and Dad's bed
and went back to her own bed. She woke
up her Dad and said, 'There's not enough
room in my bed for both of us. Sorry Dad,
but you'll have to hop out.'
Tired and bleary eyed, Dad staggered over
to Adam's bed and plonked down to sleep.

Adam was fast asleep until Boofy
started licking his face.
His licking felt sloppy and yucky.
Adam woke up and said
'Boofy you bad dog!
Boofy you pest!
I'm leaving this bed
to get some rest!'

He climbed out of his Mum and
Dad's bed and went back to his own
bed. He woke up his Dad and said,
'There's not enough room in my bed
for both of us. Sorry Dad, but you'll
have to hop out.'
Tired and bleary eyed, Dad
staggered over to Lisa's bed and
plonked down to sleep.

Lisa was fast asleep until Boofy
started nuzzling her neck.
His doggy nose felt cold and icky.
Lisa woke up and said
'Boofy you bad dog!
Boofy you pest!
I'm leaving this bed
to get some rest!'

She climbed out of her Mum and Dad's bed and went back to her own bed.
She woke up her Dad and said, 'There's not enough room in my bed for both
of us. Sorry Dad, but you'll have to
hop out.'

Tired and bleary eyed, Dad
staggered back to his own bed, put
Boofy on the floor and plonked
down next to Mum.
The lightning went flash. The
thunder went BOOM.
The wind went WOOOOH and
shook the whole room.
'Oh no!' cried Dad. 'Not again.'

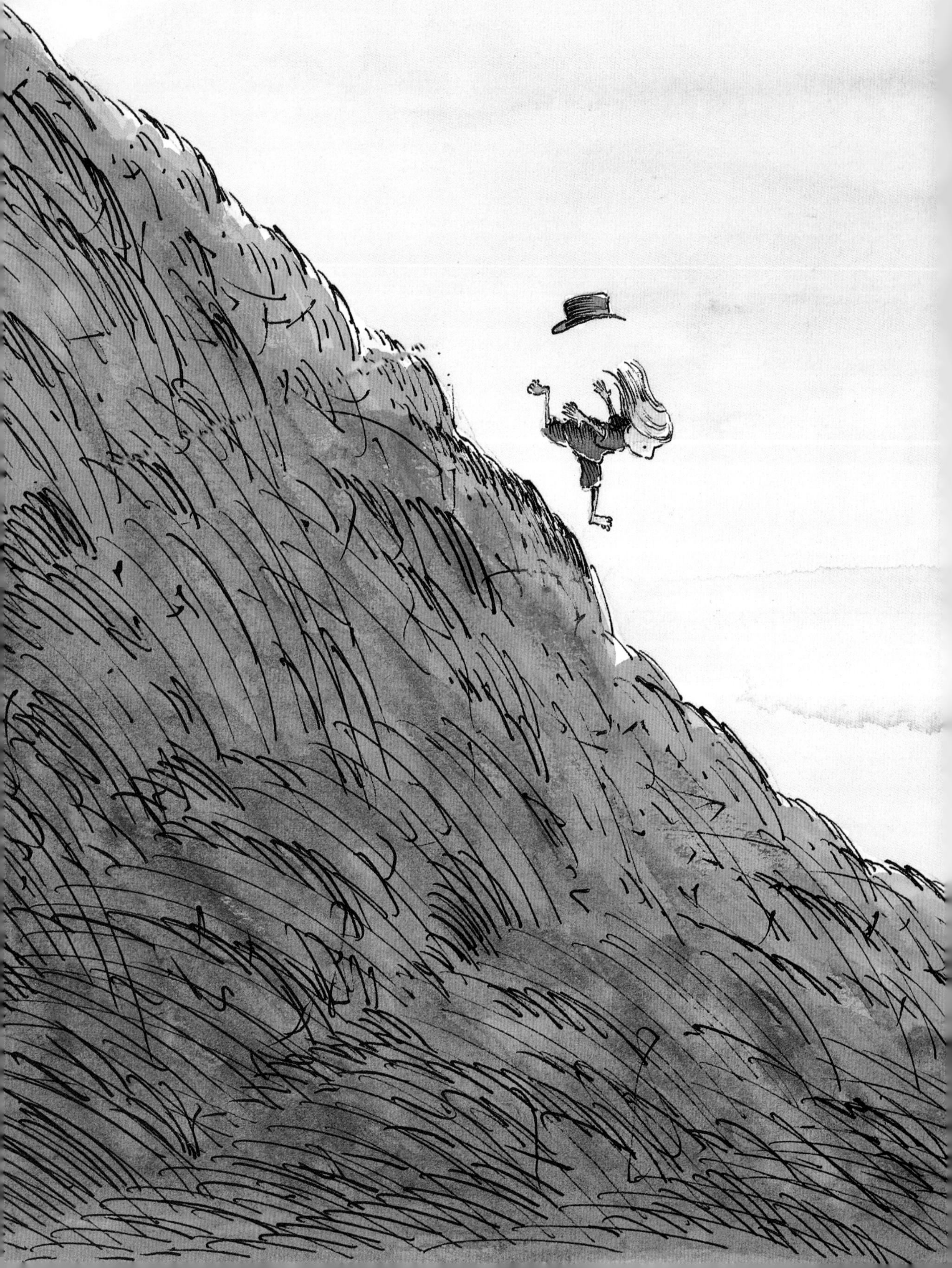

HILLS

Lydia Pender

Oh the wonderful thrill
Just to race down a hill
      When you start at the tippermost top!
Oh the glorious fun
When you've started to run,
      And you know you can't possibly stop!

Your arms are outspread,
There's a wind round your head,
      And you're certainly losing your hat!
Your heart's going thump,
And your throat's just a lump,
      Hurrah! You are down on the flat!

A SWAMP ROMP

Doug MacLeod

Clomp Thump
Swamp Lump
Plodding in the Ooze,
Belly Shiver
Jelly Quiver
Squelching in my shoes.

Clomp Thump
Romp Jump
Mulching all the Mud,
Boot Trudge
Foot Sludge
Thud! Thud! Thud!

LITTLE 'TOM THUMB'

Bill Scott

From Sydney Cove
They all set sail,
A doctor and a sailor
And a boy to bail.
Out through the Heads
And sailing south
Little 'Tom Thumb'
Left the harbour mouth.
'Tom Thumb' pitched,
'Tom Thumb' rolled,
The sea wind blew
And they all got cold.

They all got wet
With flying spray
As little 'Tom Thumb'
Sailed south-away.

They came to a beach
And stepped ashore.
The boy didn't have
To bail any more.
They dried their clothes
And made new friends
Where the south coast starts
And the east coast ends.

Then back to sea
And sailing home,
Safe to Sydney
Wet with foam.

A boy to bail,
A doctor and his chum,
Not forgetting
Little 'Tom Thumb'.

UP THE CREEK

Penny Matthews

A creek runs behind our house. At night you can hear frogs.

'Let's go exploring,' our cousin Sean said. He was staying with us for the school holidays. 'I bet no one has ever explored that creek properly before. We can observe the wildlife.'

'What wildlife?' I asked.

Sean sighed. 'There's always something, Emily,' he said. 'You just have to keep your eyes open.'

He got some bread, three apples, his binoculars and a compass, and put them all in his backpack.

I took my elephant purse with some band-aids in it, and my little brother William. Well, Mum made me take William.

William took his special toy wombat and our dog, Groucho.

Sean packed a notebook and a pencil. 'Anything can happen when you go exploring,' he said. 'You have to make a map and write everything down. Then, if you die of starvation or something, people will know what you've discovered.'

William's eyes grew big.

'Don't worry, William,' I said. 'Sean's a cub scout. He knows all about exploring.'

The creek smelled of cats, and dark trees hung over the water. William yelled when he walked into a spider web.

Sean sat down on the bank, opened his notebook, and started to draw a map.

'We'll call this part of the creek Spider Bend,' he said. 'Explorers always give names to places.' He took out his compass and squinted at it. 'We're heading due east,' he said.

William stopped yelling and looked impressed. He's only three.

After a long time we came out of the trees and into the sunshine. The creek was wider now, and orange and yellow flowers grew on its banks.

'Look, Wombat,' said William. 'Pretty.'

'We need to call this place something that means plants and things,' Sean said. 'I know—Botany Bay.'

William ran off to pick some flowers. He fell down the bank into the water. Groucho bounded after him.

There was a huge splash.

I pulled William out. Groucho did some more bounding and splashing, just for fun. Sean glared at him.

Soon the creek divided into two. There was a little island in the middle, covered with bulrushes.

Sean and I took off our boots and paddled over to the island. William kept his shoes on.

There wasn't much to see on the island. Just the bulrushes, some empty soft-drink cans and a plastic bag.

'Island of Disappointment,' Sean said. 'Let's go.'

'Wait,' I said. 'Look.' A mother duck and three ducklings were swimming out from behind the bulrushes.

'Aha!' Sean said. 'Wildlife! What did I tell you? I'll make notes.'

William was very excited. He tugged at Sean's arm. 'Bread,' he said.

Sean gave him some bread, and William threw big chunks of it into the water.

Then Groucho came racing towards us, barking like crazy, and the ducks scattered.

'Duck Inlet and Bad Dog Channel,' Sean muttered. 'I'll bet real explorers never took dogs with them.'

William started to walk backwards around the island. He tripped over a branch and scratched his leg. 'Bleeding,' he said sadly.

I put a band-aid on William's leg, and gave him a cuddle. He cried. I let him hold my elephant purse.

Sean was scribbling in his notebook. 'Sea of Blood,' he said with satisfaction. 'Never mind, William. Explorers are often hurt. They have to put up with unimaginable hardship.'

William didn't like the sound of unimaginable hardship. 'Hungry,' he snuffled. 'Want to eat.'

We sat down on the island and ate what was left of the bread, and the apples. Then we waded back over Bad Dog Channel. I had to give William a piggyback because he said his leg hurt.

The creek was really shallow now, with rocks. Bamboo grew on either side. There was rubbish everywhere.

'Perilous Passage,' yelled Sean.

We pushed our way along the bank, with the bamboo on one side and the creek on the other. Groucho trotted ahead of us until he was out of sight.

After a little while we stopped dead. A shed snakeskin lay in our path.

We stared. 'More wildlife,' Sean said. 'Pretty big wildlife.' He shivered. 'It could be a tiger snake, you know. Tiger snakes are *deadly* poisonous.'

The sun burned down.

'If there's a snakeskin,' I said, 'then where's the snake?'

There was a rustling sound in the dry bamboo leaves.

Sean whispered, 'We should make lots of noise. It's important not to show fear. I think snakes can smell fear.'

He started to stamp up and down. William and I joined in. We jumped and yelled for ages. William didn't want to stop.

'That'll show 'em,' Sean panted. 'Don't worry, William. We've frightened the snake away.'

The leaves rustled again. And then suddenly there was the loudest crashing noise.

'*Aaargh!*' screamed Sean. '*Tiger snake! Help!*'

Groucho burst out of the bamboo. He bounced up and down and grinned at us.

'Bad dog, Groucho!' I said. 'Go home! Now!'

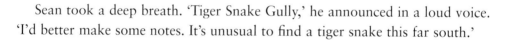

Sean took a deep breath. 'Tiger Snake Gully,' he announced in a loud voice. 'I'd better make some notes. It's unusual to find a tiger snake this far south.'

But before Sean could get out his notebook, William gave a wail that made my hair stand on end.

'*I want my wombat!*'

This was truly terrible. William couldn't do *anything* without his wombat. And what would Mum say?

'Be brave, William,' said Sean. 'Explorers don't cry.'

'They do too,' sobbed William. 'I want my wombat, and I want to go home. So there!'

Back we went up the creek to look for William's wombat. The sun grew hotter and hotter.

We found a baby lizard with a blue tongue. We found some duck eggs in an old nest, and an empty rabbit burrow beneath a blackberry bush.

But we couldn't find William's wombat anywhere. William cried and cried.

'Don't give up hope, William,' I said. 'When you're exploring, anything can happen. It's like Sean said. Remember?'

William cried even harder.

We waded back over Bad Dog Channel and paddled around to the other side of the Island of Disappointment. On the opposite creek bank willow trees reached down to the water.

I pushed aside the willow branches. Behind them was a whole new creek that opened out into a tiny lake.

And there beside the lake was—

'Groucho!' I said. 'Clever dog!'

William raced up to Groucho, grabbed his wombat and squeezed it very hard. He gave Groucho a kiss. Then he gave me a kiss.

'Look, Sean,' said William. 'Wombat!'

But Sean was staring at the new creek. '*Fantastic!*' he said. 'This is a *real* discovery. I'll bet no one has ever, ever seen this before!'

We all looked. There were dragonflies and birds and water beetles. A moorhen was poking around in the shallows. Maybe there would be yabbies. We could come back later and find out.

'We must give this creek a name,' Sean said. 'How about Sean Creek? Explorers often name places after their expedition leader.'

'No,' I said. 'We discovered it because of William's wombat. That was the best thing of all.' And I took Sean's notebook and wrote, in big letters:

WOMBAT CREEK.

THE TRAVELLER

C J Dennis

As I rode in to Burrumbeet,
I met a man with funny feet;
And, when I paused to ask him why
His feet were strange, he rolled his eye
And said the rain would spoil the wheat;
So I rode on to Burrumbeet.

As I rode in to Beetaloo,
I met a man whose nose was blue;
And, when I asked him how he got
A nose like that, he answered, 'What
Do bullocks mean when they say "Moo"?'
So I rode on to Beetaloo.

As I rode in to Ballarat,
I met a man who wore no hat;
And, when I said he might take cold,
He cried, 'The hills are quite as old
As yonder plains, but not so flat.'
So I rode on to Ballarat.

As I rode in to Gundagai,
I met a man and passed him by
Without a nod, without a word.
He turned, and said he'd never heard
Or seen a man so wise as I.
But I rode on to Gundagai.

As I rode homeward, full of doubt,
I met a stranger riding out:
A foolish man he seemed to me;
But, 'Nay, I am yourself,' said he,
'Just as you were when you rode out.'
So I rode homeward, free of doubt.

AND THE 'ROO JUMPED OVER THE MOON

D H Souter

The Kangaroo is a splendid jumper;
Short forelegs, but its tail is a thumper.

Whether it be a girl or a boy
A baby 'roo is always a joey.

Its Ma has a pocket in front of her tum
For baby to lie in, sucking its thumb.

Of all the babes that are born, but few
Have a pram like the baby kangaroo.

THE UNSOCIABLE WALLABY

C J Dennis

Willie spied a wallaby hopping through the fern—
Here a jump, here a thump, there a sudden turn.
Willie called the wallaby, begging him to stop,
But he went among the wattles with a
flip,
Flap,
FLOP!

LITTLE BROTHER POSSUM

Jane de Burgh

Little brother possum
Ventures out at night,
Nibbles at the gum-leaves,
'Cause they're nice to bite.

When the morning's coming
And the sky grows red,
Shoo! little possum,
Hurry back to bed.

IF YOU GO SOFTLY

Jenifer Kelly Flood

If you go softly out to the gum trees
At night, after the darkness falls,
If you go softly and call—
      Tch, Tch, Tch,
      Tch, Tch, Tch,
      They'll come—
          the possums!

If you take bread that you've saved
They'll come close up, and stand
And eat right from your hand—
      Softly,
      Snatching,
      Nervous—
      the possums!

And if you are still, and move slowly,
You can, very softly, pat
Their thick fur, gently, like that—
      It's true!
      You can
      Really touch them—
      the possums!

You can do that all—
  If you go softly,
    At night,
      To the gum trees,
        If you go softly
          —and call.

CICADA

Lydia Pender

Out of my way, everyone,
Out of my way!
I'm coming up, up, up, into the world today!
The world and the sun and the sky are waiting for me today!
Out of my way!

Ugly, misshapen, fat, with clawlike feet,
Clad in my overalls of dusty brown,
I lived my drab, dark life through lonely years,
Down in the drab, dark earth, deep down, deep down.

But watch! See!
This is the day, the day!
Why did not somebody say
Long, long ago—
Untold, how could I know
There was a world like this, over my head?
Would I have stayed in the grave? I am not dead!
Out of my way!

Who could have known such uninspiring shell
Would hold so rare, so exquisite a thing,
With jewelled head and dainty clinging feet
And patterned tracery of fragile wing?

See, I am ready to fly!
Breasting the sky!
This is worth all the dark years that I spent in the ground.
Ah! Let me sing, sing, sing, of the glory around!
Sing till I die!

FLYING FOXES

Lydia Pender

The Flying Foxes hang, head down,
All day, with hooded eye,
Like bags of witches' washing, strung
Along the trees to dry.

At sundown, they begin to stir
And stretch and screech and stare;
Unfold their leather wings and dive
Into the darkening air.

Like black, burnt paper-scraps they drift
Around the windy sky
To feed, and circle home, and meet,
And hook themselves on thorny feet
To sleep—almost, to die.

MAGPIES

Judith Wright

Along the road the magpies walk
with hands in pockets, left and right.
They tilt their heads, and stroll and talk.
In their well-fitted black and white

they look like certain gentlemen
who seem most nonchalant and wise
until their meal is served—and then
what clashing beaks, what greedy eyes!

But not one man that I have heard
throws back his head in such a song
of grace and praise—no man nor bird.
Their greed is brief; their joy is long.
For each is born with such a throat
as thanks his God with every note.

MRS MAG

Jean Chapman

Once upon a time, in the long ago, all the birds were busy learning bird lore. They learnt the ways of flying and what to eat. They learnt about singing. They learnt about nest-building.

But Mrs Mag, the black-and-white Australian magpie, didn't get any further than the singing. She carolled and chortled, fluted and whistled the day through. 'Listen to me, just listen to me,' she chattered happily to the other birds. 'Do listen to my beautiful voice.' Oh, she was a terrible one for opening her beak wide and boasting. Whether the others did stop to listen there's no way of knowing, but Mrs Mag sang on and on, right up to springtime.

By then the other birds were building nests. Mrs Mag knew that she should be building a nest too, but for the life of her she didn't know how.

'Tell me, tell me, tell me,' she called out, 'tell me how to build my nest!'

Luckily for her the other birds were friendly and said they'd show her how to go about it the next day.

Early in the morning, a crowd of them gathered about Mrs Mag with sticks or twigs, mud or bark, rootlets or grass, cobwebs or reeds, everything ever needed for nest-building.

'Poof! Who needs any of that stuff?' squawked the parrot.

'Not me! Neither do you, Mrs Mag,' laughed Kookaburra. Just find a hollow in a tree, as Parrot and I do. It's just the place to bring up a family.'

'A hollow tree,' chattered Mrs Mag. 'Ah yes, I knew that before.'

'A hollow tree is no place for baby plovers,' shrieked Spur-wing Plover. 'Make your nest my way, on the ground, using grass, Mrs Mag. Hide it well behind a stone or tussock.'

'Build on the ground,' warbled Mrs Mag. 'Ah yes, I knew that before.'

'Never, never, never build on the ground,' screamed Silver Gull. 'Find a high rocky cliff and make a shallow nest from seaweed. Use grass to make it soft inside if you like, Mrs Mag.'

'Use seaweed,' sang Mrs Mag, flapping a wing. 'Ah yes, I knew that before.'

'No-oo-oo-oo-oo!' hooted Tawny Frogmouth, rather sleepily, because she was a night owl. 'The safe way is to use sticks. Build a strong platform from sticks on a tree branch. Only that is safe for chicks.'

'Sticks, sticks, sticks!' fluted Mrs Mag, strutting in circle. 'Ah yes, I knew that before.'

'Not sticks!' shouted Pee-wit. 'Build in mud, wet mud. In the fork of a tree build a round mud basin. That's the nest for you, Mrs Mag.'

'Mud, mud, lovely wet mud!' trilled Mrs Mag, looking back at her tail. 'Ah yes, I knew that before.'

'Yes, yes, use mud,' shrilled Welcome Swallow, 'but your nest must be round, as round as an orange and plastered upside-down to a rock or branch.'

'As round as an orange,' Mrs Mag whistled softly and shook her tail. 'Ah yes, I knew that before.'

'Don't make a round nest whatever you do,' trilled Flame Robin. 'A cup is a better shape. Just take some bark and some grass, then fix them into a neat cup shape with a thread or so of cobweb. Do that, Mrs Mag, for a fine nest.'

'Cobweb, cobweb, cobweb!' Mrs Mag sang higher and higher, nid-nodding her head. 'Ah yes, I knew that before.'

'Cobwebs are good,' said Jacky Winter, 'so are twigs and mud, but the shape is wrong. You must build a tiny saucer of a nest, Mrs Mag. No other shape will do.'

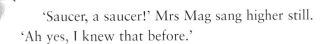

'Saucer, a saucer!' Mrs Mag sang higher still. 'Ah yes, I knew that before.'

'Now, just listen to me,' hooted Black Swan. 'Everyone else is wrong, Mrs Mag. Find a place by water, then get together some reeds and sticks. Pile 'em up and up and up into a good stack, then flop on top to flatten them down, down, down until they're good and squashed. That's the best nest for you, Mrs Mag.'

'Pile high, then squash!' carolled Mrs Mag. 'Ah yes, I knew that before.'

'Then if you know so much we can't help you,' laughed Kookaburra, and she spread her wings and flew off.

Yes, decided the other birds, Mrs Mag really didn't need any help, and away they flew.

And do you know, in next to no time, high in a tree for everyone to see, Mrs Mag had thrown together some sticks into the untidiest of nests. Then she laid two spotted eggs inside it.

The wind blew and the tree swayed but Mrs Mag stayed put in her nest.

The rain rained and the nest was soaked but Mrs Mag stayed put.

There she stayed, letting no bird or creature close to her nest, and before long two squawking little magpies were hatched.

She taught them to fly. She taught them to find food. She taught them to sing as beautifully as she did—but she could not teach them to build a tidy nest.

To this very day, every Australian magpie born is unable to build a nest any better than the rough bundle of sticks Mrs Mag flung together long ago, but they can all sing. Ah yes, they can sing!

NIGHT BIRDS

Geoffrey Dutton

I wonder why
Birds sing by day, but at night they cry.

The curlews wail
As if they hope to find, but fail.

Oyster-catchers echo
Each other as if the beach were hollow.

The mopoke calls
How far away the darkness falls.

The rainbird spills
Notes into a dam that never fills.

Only the magpie
By moonlight sings and does not cry.

A SHORT, SUMMERY THIN THONG SONG

Max Fatchen

The song
of a
thong
is a flip,
flap,
flong
that echoes
wherever
you go.
There aren't
any places
for silly
old laces
but a thing
that holds
on to
your toe.

You're flapping
and tapping
with feet
overlapping
and people who watch
will agree
that the song
of a thong
when you're
flopping along
is of feet
that are born
to be
free.

STATUE

Sally Odgers

In the summer days I run
Down to the hem of the sea,
I lie in the sand and let the waves
Come washing over me.

Salt and wet
I roll and roll
Then straight and still I stand.
People passing think they see
A statue made of sand.

THE SEA

Lilith Norman

Deep glass-green seas
chew rocks
with their green-glass jaws.
But little waves
creep in
and nibble softly at the sand.

THE ROCK POOL

Peter Skrzynecki

The rock pool
is a magic circle
full of colours the sea
washes in—
blues, greens, browns, reds:
yellow that leaps
in reflection
and does a somersault
over your head!

Seagrass weaves
in slow, soft dances—
reaches up to your face
and hands:
growing out of tiny pebbles
and the patterns
of drifting sand.

Here's a crab
that scuttles sideways,
hiding under a shelf of stone.
Look—here's a fish
with purple stripes!
And—there—
a piece of cuttlebone.

The rock pool
is a magic circle
full of treasures
from a sea king's cave—
thrown up for the delight
of children
by swirling tide
and crashing waves!

EVENING

Colin Thiele

I like to see
At end of day
The setting sun's
Last shining ray;

And hear the note
A late bird sings
As shadows fall
Like folding wings;

And see this gift
Of priceless worth—
A gentle peace
Upon the earth.

ACKNOWLEDGEMENTS

The compiler and publisher are grateful for permission to include the following copyright material:

Anne Bell for 'The Caretakers', 'The Little Things' and 'On Rainy Nights' all first published in the NSW Department of Education *School Magazine*.

Jean Chapman for 'Mrs Mag'.

Peter Combe for 'Please Wash Me Up'.

Geoffrey Dutton: Curtis Brown (Australia) Pty Ltd for 'Night Birds'.

Libby Hathorn for 'There and Back'.

Nan Hunt for 'The Hippolottamuss' first published in *Can I Keep Him?: Stories About Pets*, Oxford University Press, 1991.

Robin Klein: Haytul Pty Ltd, c/o Curtis Brown (Australia) Pty Ltd for 'Rainbow Duckling'.

Norman Lindsay: HarperCollins Publishers for 'It's Worse than Weevils' first published in *The Magic Pudding*, Angus & Robertson, 1918.

Gwendda McKay: 'Morning and Evening' first published in *Big Dipper Returns*, Oxford University Press, 1985; 'The Sock Funeral' first published in *Big Dipper Rides Again*, Oxford University Press, 1982, both by permission of the editors.

Doug MacLeod: Penguin Books Australia for 'A Swamp Song', first published in *In the Garden of Bad Things*, 1981.

Lilith Norman for 'The Sea', and for 'The King who Wanted to Reach the Moon'.

Sally Odgers for 'Statue'.

Pixie O'Harris: Curtis Brown (Australia) Pty Ltd for 'Wouldn't it be Funny'.

Lydia Pender for 'Dan McDougall and the Bulldozer' first published by Abelard Schuman 1963; 'Cicada' and 'Hills' both first published in *Morning Magpie*, Angus and Robertson, 1984; 'Flying Foxes' first published in *The Land and the Spirit: an Australian Alphabet*, Margaret Hamilton Books, 1992, all reprinted by permission of the author.

Dorothy Rickards: 'City Song' first published in *Big Dipper*, Oxford University Press, 1980, by permission of the editors.

Bill Scott for 'Little "Tom Thumb"' first published in *Brother and Brother*, Jacaranda Press, 1972.

Joan M Shilton: 'Coming Home' and 'Gardening Home' both first published in *Big Dipper Rides Again*, Oxford University Press, 1992, by permission of the editors.

Dorothy Simmons for 'Who'll Buy?', first published as 'Puppies for Sale' in Sunshine Magazine, 1992 by Wendy Pye Pty Ltd.

Peter Skrzynecki for 'The Rock Pool'.

Colin Thiele for 'The Bathroom Bunyip', 'Evening' and 'Watching Eye' all first published in *Poems in my Luggage*, Omnibus Books, 1989.

Gordon Winch for 'Too Early'.

Judith Wright: HarperCollins Publishers for 'Magpies' from *Collected Poems*.

Every effort has been made to locate copyright holders. In the case of any omissions, the publisher will be pleased to make acknowledgements in future editions.